FAMILY PRACTICES

A Guided Journal of Togetherness and Discovery with Your Loved Ones

Janine Wilburn

WEST
MARGIN
PRESS

This Journal Is Ours

It contains our hopes and dreams
Our love and kindnesses
Our laughter and joy
Our appreciation and gratitude
Our acts of forgiveness and service
Our shared values, purpose, and mission...
All captured here for us to use.

This journal belongs to

The _____ Family

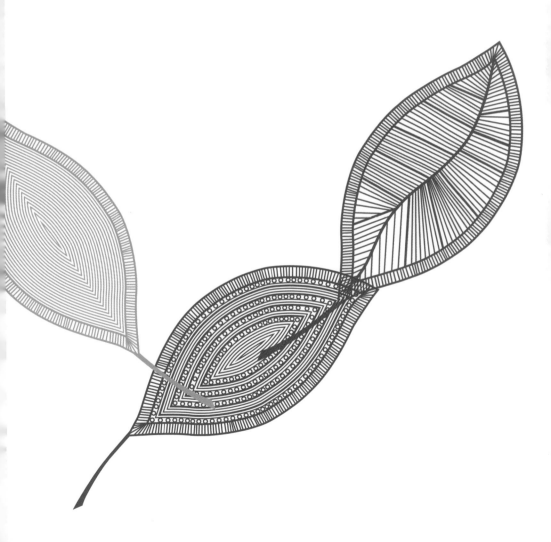

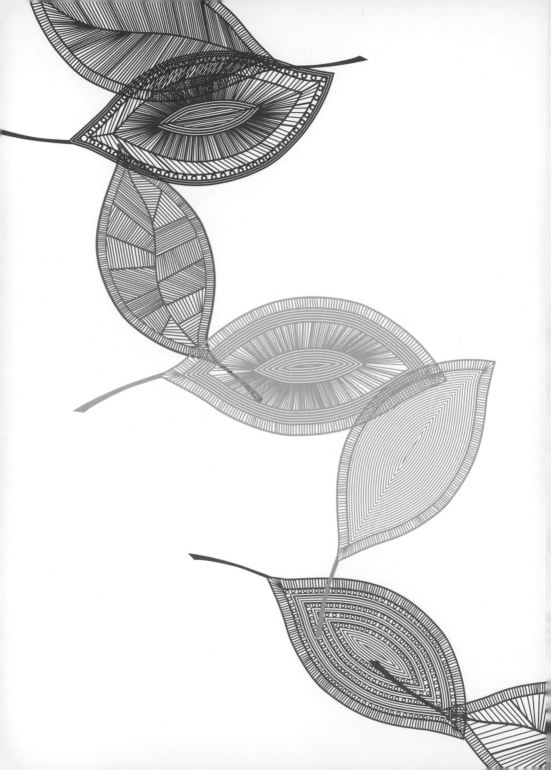

CONTENTS

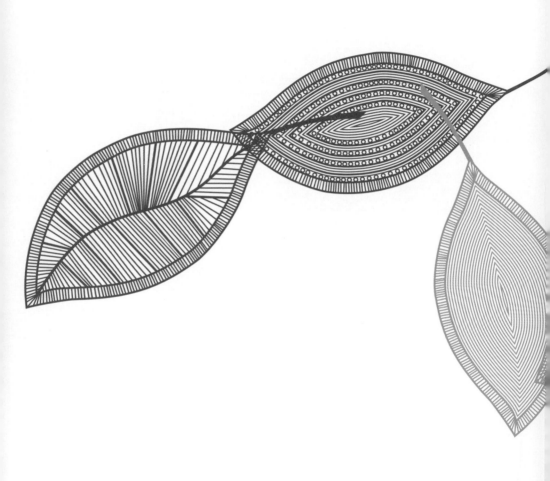

INTRODUCTION

Welcome to the *Family Practices* journal! This book is about having fun and creating connections within your family while engaging everyone in entertaining, relationship-strengthening, inspiring, and thought-provoking activities that are the building blocks of resilience. While heartwarming and approachable, every activity is developed based on research, study, and experience, making this book both fun and good for you. So, let's get started.

What Is Resilience? Resilience is the ability to recover quickly from difficulties and challenges—to be tough, strong, and sturdy as well as flexible, durable, and buoyant. Resilience is the capacity some people, adults and children, have to cope in a positive way to the inevitable challenges of life. Resilient people survive the most difficult physical, emotional, and mentally challenging experiences to thrive, whereas other people experience similar situations or circumstances and never recover.

Can You Learn Resilience, or Are You Just Born with It? The good news is that you can build your resiliency. An area of neuroscience called neuroplasticity has engaged scientists, philosophers, doctors, and therapists around the world in studying why some people are more resilient than others. In studying neuroplasticity, it is common to connect what has once been seen as softer, even spiritual principles to science, using research to explain the changes in the brain and body based on changes in thought. These new discoveries reveal the brain is more malleable than previously understood, and even subtle changes can create new neuropathways that assist in building resilience. The research further reveals that resilience is a skill developed on the physical, emotional, and mental levels, and that by choosing specific thought patterns, behaviors, and physical activities, adults and children can become more resilient.

What Is the Value of Building Resiliency? The value of resiliency lies in the ability to survive what would seem to be devastating experiences, as well as the ability to move through the day without being adversely affected by life's inevitable upward and downward swings. For example, imagine a teenager who can routinely create optimism, authentic self-esteem, and positivity in the face of peer pressure, adolescent changes, and educational demands. Consider the benefits of connection and communication for a family who shares resilience tools and practices as they deal with their collective and individual daily stressors. Research shows that being resilient helps make day-to-day issues lighter and the traumatic experiences handleable.

Where Do I Find Resiliency? With the help of brain imaging technology, the science around neuroplasticity has proven that all of us can increase our resiliency through choosing specific types of thought patterns, behaviors, and physical activities. Focused research on the subject has identified a variety of resiliency-building skills, including staying connected, being creative, taking care of others, being grateful, letting go through forgiveness, having a purpose, being of service, and expressing love. Developing regular, ideally daily, practices in any of these areas will help create new neuropathways and bolster resilience. This journal will guide your family through activities to do just that.

So, Why Should You Care? Being resilient makes life easier and more fun, while also helping to reduce upsets and downward spirals when dealing with stress and challenges. It helps you to achieve your goals and dreams as you have the resilience to never give up. Importantly, you can use it for your entire life as resilience never wears out or gets old.

How Do I Know?

Resiliency plays a critical role in my daily life and in my family's life. Twenty-four years ago, I was in a serious car accident. I experienced severe spinal injuries and was given a grim prognosis. This was when I first encountered this new distinction in neuroscience called neuroplasticity, through Sharon Begley's book *Train Your Mind, Change Your Brain* and her exploration of Dr. Richard Davidson's research at the University of Wisconsin-Madison (my alma mater). I read and reread the book, and then studied everything I could find on the subject. I knew there were answers in the science to help me heal when most of my doctors and health care practitioners no longer believed it was possible.

I began to engage and develop daily practices that eventually were identified through research as the building blocks of resiliency. The results were overwhelmingly positive. My pain started to diminish, and sleep was available for a few hours at a time. I discovered that by being creative I could significantly minimize my pain, so I became a visual artist, even though I had limited use of my hands and arms at the time.

I dug deeper into observing, monitoring, and utilizing my thoughts to enhance my healing, and combined that knowledge and intention to create my many daily practices. In pursuit of a "cure," I found so much more. I learned the importance of love when dealing with hardship. I learned love comes in so many shapes and sizes: forgiveness, gratitude, kindness, creativity, acts of service, authentic listening, compassion, daily practices, prayer, meditation, yoga, still and quiet moments, exercise, and healthy eating.

Although my sought-after "return to normal" has not materialized, I am deeply grateful.

I have learned so much, gained so much knowledge and maybe a little wisdom. I learned a new definition of hope—our only opportunity for control. That real, open-hearted connection is critical; that gratitude is one of our greatest tools; and that being of service is one of our greatest gifts. I learned to never stop trying and to never give up. I learned to appreciate every day and work to be present and conscious in the moment.

I have so much—my family who inspires me every day, my dedicated teachers who continue to support me, the people who allow me to be of service in their lives, my daily practices, and the many, many aspects of love. All these help me to continuously create and shape a life I love and am passionate about. I learned we never really know what the next moment or twenty-four years have in store for us; however, with our minds and our practices, we can make it something special.

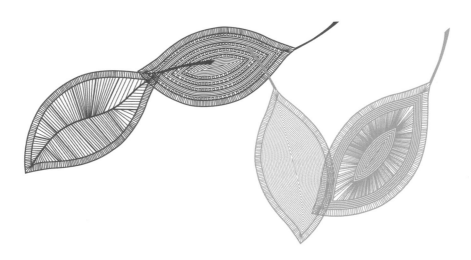

How to Use This Book

This journal provides a series of actions that help bring families together. Things change and sometimes moving forward can be confusing or even a little daunting. *Family Practices* engages families in the thoughts, actions, and practices that are the very underpinnings of resilience. It contains a number of different types of exercises—all designed to work together to help create connection, strengthen relationships, and build resiliency for the family and each family member. There are activities to be filled out individually and with the whole family. For family activities, designate one person to write down all the contributions or pass it around so everyone who wants to write for the family gets an opportunity to do so.

Every section's activities are based on a distinct resiliency-building action. As you absorb yourselves in the fun, it is your turn to create, contemplate, connect, and communicate using these tools that science now proves to make people more emotionally, mentally, and physically resilient.

So, follow along. There is not a right or wrong way to complete this journal. You can select specific weekdays to journal, and you can include the journaling in daily activities such as after mealtimes, before bed, or during long car rides. You can also leave the journal out in a place where you'll see it and work on it whenever you feel like it. The most valuable thing is to engage with the different activities. Decide which tools you like the best and use them. It starts here and now, so dream, vision, and create. Anything is possible!

TIPS FOR FAMILIES

- Use the tools in the journal to help you get to know each other better.

- Take time to listen to each other. Just five minutes every day of uninterrupted listening to a family member helps build resiliency and relationships.

- Make it a habit to appreciate or thank every person in your family at least once a day.

- Support everyone getting some exercise every day. A little can go a long way, if you do it every day.

- Tell each other about daily acts of kindness you've seen or experienced.

- Share with each other how you helped someone and how someone helped you.

- Do at least one family activity a week. This can be as simple as singing a song together.

- Most importantly, remember to say *I love you, You're important to me, I'm sorry,* and *I forgive you.*

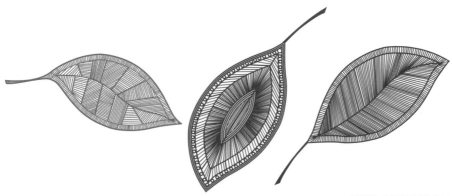

*The most precious gift
we can offer others is our
presence. When mindfulness
embraces those we love,
they will bloom like flowers.*
—Thich Nhat Hanh

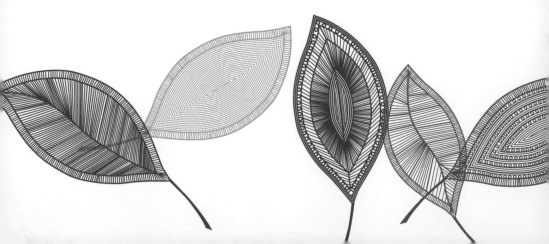

CONNECTION

Spread love everywhere you go:
First of all in your own house...
Let no one ever come to you
without leaving better and
happier. Be the living expression
of kindness; kindness in your
face, kindness in your eyes,
kindness in your smile, kindness
in your warm greeting.

—Mother Teresa

Our Family

Resilient families are built on love, communication, caring, and connection. In this section, you will be asked to capture specifics about yourselves and your family. Research reveals that connection comes through the sharing of everyday moments as much as special memories and accomplishments. They all combine to construct your foundation. Share from your heart and enjoy the journey.

WHO WE ARE

These two pages are designed to be completed
together, as a family. Designate one person to fill in
the journal as the others share their strengths, skills,
and special ways they contribute to the family.

PERSON	STRENGTHS	SKILLS

HOW WE CONTRIBUTE

PERSON	SPECIAL CONTRIBUTIONS
_____	_____
_____	_____
_____	_____
_____	_____
_____	_____
_____	_____
_____	_____
_____	_____
_____	_____
_____	_____
_____	_____
_____	_____
_____	_____
_____	_____
_____	_____
_____	_____

TOGETHER OUR FAMILY IS...

Circle the words that best describe your family's qualities. You could also use the empty space to add more words.

FUNNY *Delightful* **Strong**

Sharing **Brave**

CURIOUS **Innovative** UPBEAT

Creative PROSPEROUS

Talented VITAL Humorous

Joyful Blessed

Playful Problem Solving **Silly**

BEAUTIFUL **ENTHUSIASTIC**

SECURE *Loving* **Healthy**

Happy GENTLE

TOGETHER OUR FAMILY BELIEVES IN...

Circle the words that best describe your family's values. Use the empty space to add any of your values that aren't listed.

Honoring commitments   **Acting with purpose**

Pursuing one's dreams   **Giving generously**

ACTING BOLDLY   Encouraging others

BEING KIND   *Remaining optimistic*

Being inspired and being inspiring   Working hard

Being accepting   BEING OF SERVICE

Being positive   BEING GENEROUS

Lending a helping hand   *Expressing gratitude*

BEING THOUGHTFUL

OUR SHARED EVERYDAY MOMENTS

Research reveals that connection comes through sharing the "everyday moments." Telling each other about routine daily activities helps build bonds, deepens understanding, and creates feelings of closeness.

List some of your daily updates that you regularly share with each other.

-
-
-
-
-
-
-
-
-
-
-
-

OUR SPECIAL FAMILY DAYS

Fill in the space below with special family activities. For example: *Fresh Fruit Fridays, Movie Mondays, Hiking on the Weekends,* or *Binge Watching Shows.*

-
-
-
-
-
-
-
-
-
-
-
-
-
-
-

CELEBRATING OUR WAY

Fill in these pages with your favorite family holidays and traditions. Remember the big things and the little things that you do to make each day uniquely yours.

HOLIDAY: _____

OUR TRADITIONS: _____

_____

_____

HOLIDAY: _____

OUR TRADITIONS: _____

_____

_____

HOLIDAY: _____

OUR TRADITIONS: _____

_____

_____

HOLIDAY: _____

OUR TRADITIONS: _____

_____

_____

HOLIDAY: _____

OUR TRADITIONS: _____

_____

_____

HOLIDAY: _____

OUR TRADITIONS: _____

_____

_____

HOLIDAY: _____

OUR TRADITIONS: _____

_____

_____

HOLIDAY: _____

OUR TRADITIONS: _____

_____

_____

HOLIDAY: _____

OUR TRADITIONS: _____

_____

_____

OUR FAVORITES

Here is the space to record your best-loved family stories—those unforgettable narratives told with love, humor, compassion, joy, and even some facts.

BEST MEMORIES

_____

_____

_____

_____

_____

_____

_____

FUNNIEST MEMORIES

_____

_____

_____

_____

_____

_____

_____

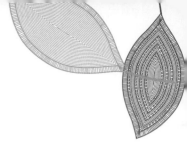

MOST UNFORGETTABLE MEMORIES

_____

_____

_____

_____

_____

_____

_____

HAPPIEST MEMORIES

_____

_____

_____

_____

_____

_____

_____

OUR FAVORITES

Capture your shared and individual bests of each category in these next pages. Ties are allowed. So, if your family has more than one absolute favorite movie or show or book, that is perfectly okay.

TOP TEN MOVIES

1) _____   6) _____

2) _____   7) _____

3) _____   8) _____

4) _____   9) _____

5) _____   10) _____

TOP TEN SHOWS

1) _____   6) _____

2) _____   7) _____

3) _____   8) _____

4) _____   9) _____

5) _____   10) _____

TOP TEN BOOKS

1) _____
2) _____
3) _____
4) _____
5) _____
6) _____
7) _____
8) _____
9) _____
10) _____

TOP TEN _____

1) _____
2) _____
3) _____
4) _____
5) _____
6) _____
7) _____
8) _____
9) _____
10) _____

OUR FAVORITES

Here is the place to record all your favorite foods and meals, homemade or otherwise.

PERSON   FAVORITE FOODS & MEALS

_____   _____

_____   _____

_____   _____

_____   _____

_____   _____

_____   _____

_____   _____

_____   _____

_____   _____

_____   _____

_____   _____

_____   _____

_____   _____

_____   _____

_____   _____

_____   _____

_____   _____

Whether it is ice cream, cookies, cupcakes, or chocolates, we all have a chosen indulgence. List yours below. This is a good page to look at when you want to do a little something nice for someone in your family.

PERSON

FAVORITE SWEETS & TREATS

_____   _____

_____   _____

_____   _____

_____   _____

_____   _____

_____   _____

_____   _____

_____   _____

_____   _____

_____   _____

_____   _____

_____   _____

_____   _____

_____   _____

*Laugh often, dream big,
reach for the stars.*

—Unknown

Family Fun

Family fun comes in all shapes and sizes. It can be meticulously planned or pop up unexpectedly. Remembering, revisiting and reliving those times helps strengthen the bonds between loved ones. It is also really entertaining! Enjoy yourselves as you fill out this section.

TEN THINGS THAT MAKE US SMILE

1) _____

2) _____

3) _____

4) _____

5) _____

6) _____

7) _____

8) _____

9) _____

10) _____

TEN THINGS THAT MAKE US LAUGH

1) _____

2) _____

3) _____

4) _____

5) _____

6) _____

7) _____

8) _____

9) _____

10) _____

TEN THINGS WE LIKE TO DO TOGETHER

1) _____

2) _____

3) _____

4) _____

5) _____

6) _____

7) _____

8) _____

9) _____

10) _____

TEN THINGS THAT GIVE US JOY

1) _____

2) _____

3) _____

4) _____

5) _____

6) _____

7) _____

8) _____

9) _____

10) _____

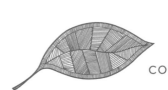

Imagination is more important than knowledge. Knowledge is limited. Imagination encircles the world.

—Albert Einstein

Being Creative

The act of being creative is another one of those powerful gifts that is often misunderstood. We grow up believing we need to have "talent" to be an artist, actor, dancer, musician, singer, chef, or the like. However, being creative is not about the end result, it is about the act itself. Releasing ourselves into a creative endeavor allows us to regenerate, relax, and regroup. It is the perfect anecdote to a stressful day. It is a favorite resiliency tool. Ending up with a final product that you like is a bonus.

CREATING TOGETHER

Circle creative activities that you like to do individually and/or together. If there is something you enjoy that isn't on the list, add it!

- Coloring inside the lines
- Coloring outside the lines
- Acting
- Painting
- Collaging
- Dancing
- Singing
- Sewing
- Printmaking
- Baking

- Cake decorating
- Storytelling
- Drawing
- Writing
- Sketching
- Filmmaking
- Photography
- Gardening
- Reading
- Scrapbooking

Now, select a creative project for your family to do from the list below or create your own project. Choose something you like to do or something you've always wanted to try. You can make it as simple or elaborate as you want. Remember, it is the act of creating that is most valuable; the end product is the bonus.

- Invent a new game
- Perform a play
- Devise your own language
- Make up silly songs
- Choreograph a dance
- Create finger & hand puppets
- Develop a storytelling group
- Make a family photobook
- Paint a mural
- Write a story

- Bake the best cookies
- Make signs & posters
- Face paint
- Write poems
- Plant a garden
- Conduct science experiments
- Compose original songs
- Write your family story
- Create a family cookbook

CREATING TOGETHER

Write a story together using the following words. Have each person write one line, and repeat until the page is filled. Then read the story together with each person reading their line(s).

Today _____

joyfully _____

red stickers _____

watermelon _____

happy dance _____

click, click _____

the birds _____

candlestick _____

rubber boots _____

and my favorite hat _____

THE SUPERHERO VERSION OF OUR FAMILY

Create your superhero family using favorite known heroes as well as heroes from your imaginations. Name each person as a superhero and list their special superhero powers.

SUPERHERO   SPECIAL POWERS

_____   _____

_____   _____

_____   _____

_____   _____

_____   _____

_____   _____

_____   _____

_____   _____

_____   _____

_____   _____

_____   _____

_____   _____

_____   _____

_____   _____

_____   _____

Each of us has a spark of life inside us, and our highest endeavor ought to be to set off that spark in one another.

—Kenny Ausubel

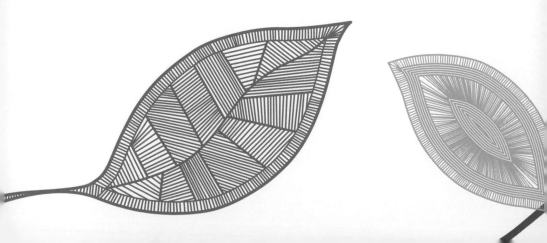

TAKING CARE OF EACH OTHER

When we seek to discover the best in others, we somehow bring out the best in ourselves.

—William Arthur Ward

The Importance of Appreciation

Everyone loves to be appreciated for what they do. It is important to take a few moments to frequently recognize and thank everyone in your family.

FAMILY APPRECIATION AWARDS

In this section, recognize each other for all your many talents, characteristics, and contributions. It feels good to be seen and valued, so be generous in your acknowledgments. Some awards might go to everyone, and that is exactly right!

AND THE APPRECIATION AWARD GOES TO...

THE FUNNIEST PEOPLE IN OUR FAMILY

_____

_____

_____

THE KINDEST PEOPLE IN OUR FAMILY

_____

_____

_____

THE SILLIEST PEOPLE IN OUR FAMILY

_____

_____

_____

THE HARDEST WORKERS IN OUR FAMILY

_____

_____

_____

THE BRAVEST PEOPLE IN OUR FAMILY

_____

_____

_____

AND THE APPRECIATION AWARD GOES TO...

THE WITTIEST PEOPLE IN OUR FAMILY
_____
_____
_____

THE STRONGEST PEOPLE IN OUR FAMILY
_____
_____
_____

THE HAPPIEST PEOPLE IN OUR FAMILY
_____
_____
_____

THE NICEST PEOPLE IN OUR FAMILY
_____
_____
_____

THE CALMEST PEOPLE IN OUR FAMILY
_____
_____
_____

AND THE APPRECIATION AWARD GOES TO...

THE MOST GIVING PEOPLE IN OUR FAMILY

_____
_____
_____

THE MOST CONSIDERATE PEOPLE IN OUR FAMILY

_____
_____
_____
_____

THE MOST HELPFUL PEOPLE IN OUR FAMILY

_____
_____
_____

THE MOST FORGIVING PEOPLE IN OUR FAMILY

_____
_____
_____

THE MOST LOVING PEOPLE IN OUR FAMILY

_____
_____
_____

AND THE APPRECIATION AWARD GOES TO...

THE MOST CREATIVE PEOPLE IN OUR FAMILY

_____

_____

_____

THE MOST INNOVATIVE PEOPLE IN OUR FAMILY

_____

_____

_____

THE MOST GRATEFUL PEOPLE IN OUR FAMILY

_____

_____

_____

THE MOST ENERGETIC PEOPLE IN OUR FAMILY

_____

_____

_____

THE MOST MUSICAL PEOPLE IN OUR FAMILY

_____

_____

_____

CREATE YOUR OWN AWARDS

You know your family best. Create awards to thank, appreciate, and recognize each other. Fill these pages in one sitting or over time. Revisit them regularly as a family and individually to remind yourselves just how loved you are.

THE MOST _____ PEOPLE IN OUR FAMILY
_____
_____
_____

THE MOST _____ PEOPLE IN OUR FAMILY
_____
_____
_____

THE MOST _____ PEOPLE IN OUR FAMILY
_____
_____
_____

THE MOST _____ PEOPLE IN OUR FAMILY
_____
_____
_____

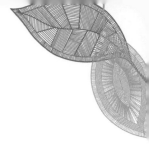

THE MOST _____ PEOPLE IN OUR FAMILY
_____
_____
_____

THE MOST _____ PEOPLE IN OUR FAMILY
_____
_____
_____

THE MOST _____ PEOPLE IN OUR FAMILY
_____
_____
_____

THE MOST _____ PEOPLE IN OUR FAMILY
_____
_____
_____

Gratitude unlocks the fullness of life. It turns what we have into enough, and more. It turns denial into acceptance, chaos to order, confusion to clarity. It can turn a meal into a feast, a house into a home, a stranger into a friend... Gratitude makes sense of our past, brings peace for today, and creates a vision for tomorrow.

—Melody Beattie

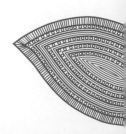

The Gift of Gratitude

The power of gratitude is almost incomprehensible as it seems to be such a simple act of acknowledgment. Gratitude has the ability to help us melt away challenges by positively shifting our perspective, enhancing our well-being, and building resiliency. In fact, studies show gratitude can be used to help with mood swings, anxiety, and even post-traumatic stress.

However, gratitude is not always an easy practice. When facing overwhelming difficulties and deep loss, reaching for gratitude can feel more challenging than climbing Mount Everest. That is why it is critical to understand gratitude is not just an emotion; it is a tool that brings peace, even happiness, when confronting pain and loss.

Note your gratefulness for anything and everything, from pizza to world peace. Since gratitude is a state of being and not a feeling, you can repeat gratitude statements when you're upset, angry, or hurt as well as when you are happy. You can express gratitude over things that have happened. You can also express gratitude over things you would like to happen. These are called gratitude intentions. There is no right or wrong way to be grateful or to do gratitude. The important thing is to do it.

OUR FAMILY GRATITUDE LIST

Fill out these lists as a group with someone writing the gratitudes in the book, or pass the book around for each family member to fill in individually. Remember, nothing is too small to be grateful for.

WE ARE GRATEFUL FOR _____

WE ARE GRATEFUL FOR _____

WE ARE GRATEFUL FOR _____

WE ARE GRATEFUL FOR _____

WE ARE GRATEFUL FOR _____

WE ARE GRATEFUL FOR _____

WE ARE GRATEFUL FOR _____

WE ARE GRATEFUL FOR _____

WE ARE GRATEFUL FOR _____

WE ARE GRATEFUL FOR _____

OUR FAMILY GRATITUDE LIST

WE ARE GRATEFUL FOR _____

WE ARE GRATEFUL FOR _____

WE ARE GRATEFUL FOR _____

WE ARE GRATEFUL FOR _____

WE ARE GRATEFUL FOR _____

WE ARE GRATEFUL FOR _____

WE ARE GRATEFUL FOR _____

WE ARE GRATEFUL FOR _____

WE ARE GRATEFUL FOR _____

WE ARE GRATEFUL FOR _____

WE ARE GRATEFUL FOR _____

WE ARE GRATEFUL FOR _____

NICE THINGS OTHERS HAVE DONE FOR US

It is uplifting to remember what others have done for our family or family members. Together, record those important moments, and continue adding to your lists over time.

-
-
-
-
-
-
-
-
-
-

NICE THINGS OTHERS HAVE DONE FOR US

-
-
-
-
-
-
-
-
-
-

BEING GRATEFUL FOR EACH OTHER

Here is the space to record what you are most grateful for from your family members, including them just being there. Over these pages, each family member can write gratitudes about every other family member. For example: *I am grateful for Luke for making me laugh.* You can do this together as a group or individually.

I AM GRATEFUL FOR _____

I AM GRATEFUL FOR _____

I AM GRATEFUL FOR _____

I AM GRATEFUL FOR _____

I AM GRATEFUL FOR _____

I AM GRATEFUL FOR _____

I AM GRATEFUL FOR _____

I AM GRATEFUL FOR _____

I AM GRATEFUL FOR _____

I AM GRATEFUL FOR _____

BEING GRATEFUL FOR EACH OTHER

I AM GRATEFUL FOR _____

I AM GRATEFUL FOR _____

I AM GRATEFUL FOR _____

I AM GRATEFUL FOR _____

I AM GRATEFUL FOR _____

I AM GRATEFUL FOR _____

I AM GRATEFUL FOR _____

I AM GRATEFUL FOR _____

I AM GRATEFUL FOR _____

I AM GRATEFUL FOR _____

FAMILY GRATITUDE INTENTIONS

These gratitude lists are different from the ones you just completed. Here, as a family, you will complete gratitude statements for what you desire in your lives as if it currently exists. For example, if you are looking for a new place to live, you would write: *We are grateful for our new home.* Reread your gratitude intentions regularly and keep adding to them over time.

WE ARE GRATEFUL FOR _____

WE ARE GRATEFUL FOR _____

WE ARE GRATEFUL FOR _____

WE ARE GRATEFUL FOR _____

WE ARE GRATEFUL FOR _____

WE ARE GRATEFUL FOR _____

WE ARE GRATEFUL FOR _____

WE ARE GRATEFUL FOR _____

WE ARE GRATEFUL FOR _____

WE ARE GRATEFUL FOR _____

FAMILY GRATITUDE INTENTIONS

WE ARE GRATEFUL FOR _____

WE ARE GRATEFUL FOR _____

WE ARE GRATEFUL FOR _____

WE ARE GRATEFUL FOR _____

WE ARE GRATEFUL FOR _____

WE ARE GRATEFUL FOR _____

WE ARE GRATEFUL FOR _____

WE ARE GRATEFUL FOR _____

WE ARE GRATEFUL FOR _____

WE ARE GRATEFUL FOR _____

FAMILY GRATITUDE INTENTIONS

Continue writing gratitude statements for what you desire in your lives as if it currently exists. Reread your gratitude intentions regularly and keep adding to them over time.

WE ARE GRATEFUL FOR _____

WE ARE GRATEFUL FOR _____

WE ARE GRATEFUL FOR _____

WE ARE GRATEFUL FOR _____

WE ARE GRATEFUL FOR _____

WE ARE GRATEFUL FOR _____

WE ARE GRATEFUL FOR _____

WE ARE GRATEFUL FOR _____

WE ARE GRATEFUL FOR _____

WE ARE GRATEFUL FOR _____

FAMILY GRATITUDE INTENTIONS

WE ARE GRATEFUL FOR _____

WE ARE GRATEFUL FOR _____

WE ARE GRATEFUL FOR _____

WE ARE GRATEFUL FOR _____

WE ARE GRATEFUL FOR _____

WE ARE GRATEFUL FOR _____

WE ARE GRATEFUL FOR _____

WE ARE GRATEFUL FOR _____

WE ARE GRATEFUL FOR _____

WE ARE GRATEFUL FOR _____

PERSONAL GRATITUDE INTENTIONS

Capture what you envision having in your individual lives and write your gratitude intentions as if they are already present. If this practice feels too private to share, write down your gratitude intentions on a piece of paper, in a book, or in your phone. Keep your gratitude intentions handy so you can read them daily and keep adding to them.

MY NAME _____

I AM GRATEFUL FOR _____

_____

_____

_____

_____

MY NAME _____

I AM GRATEFUL FOR _____

_____

_____

_____

_____

MY NAME _____

I AM GRATEFUL FOR _____

_____

_____

_____

_____

MY NAME _____

I AM GRATEFUL FOR _____

_____

_____

_____

_____

MY NAME _____

I AM GRATEFUL FOR _____

_____

_____

_____

_____

PERSONAL GRATITUDE INTENTIONS

Continue to capture what you envision having in your individual lives and write your gratitude intentions as if they are already present. Keep your gratitude intentions handy so you can read them daily and keep adding to them.

MY NAME _____

I AM GRATEFUL FOR _____

_____

_____

_____

_____

MY NAME _____

I AM GRATEFUL FOR _____

_____

_____

_____

_____

MY NAME _____

I AM GRATEFUL FOR _____

_____

_____

_____

_____

MY NAME _____

I AM GRATEFUL FOR _____

_____

_____

_____

_____

MY NAME _____

I AM GRATEFUL FOR _____

_____

_____

_____

_____

The practice of forgiveness
is our most important
contribution to the
healing of the world.

—Marianne Williamson

The Fun of Forgiveness

Forgiveness is another one of those incredibly powerful tools. It is a gift to each and every one of us. It gives us freedom to move forward unencumbered. Whether we are forgiving ourselves or someone else, forgiveness allows us to let go of the hurt, anger, and upset, and to heal. Being able to forgive also helps us build resilience. Forgiveness is not always easy, but with practice it can become so.

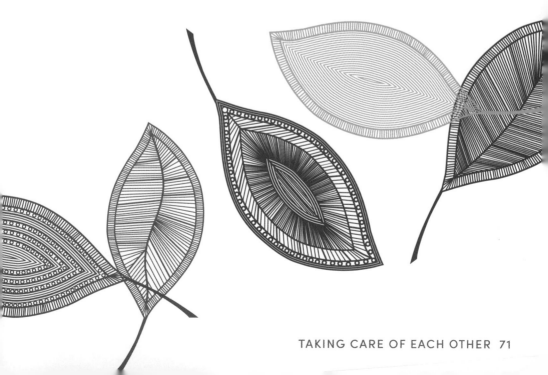

FORGIVENESS GIFTS

You can fill in the forgiveness gifts together as a family or individually. Choose the way you feel most comfortable to complete this exercise.

I, _____, FORGIVE _____
_____
_____

I, _____, FORGIVE _____
_____
_____

I, _____, FORGIVE _____
_____
_____

I, _____, FORGIVE _____
_____
_____

I, _____, FORGIVE _____
_____
_____

I, _____, FORGIVE _____

_____

_____

I, _____, FORGIVE _____

_____

_____

I, _____, FORGIVE _____

_____

_____

I, _____, FORGIVE _____

_____

_____

I, _____, FORGIVE _____

_____

_____

FORGIVENESS GIFTS

I, _____, FORGIVE _____
_____
_____

I, _____, FORGIVE _____
_____
_____

I, _____, FORGIVE _____
_____
_____

I, _____, FORGIVE _____
_____
_____

I, _____, FORGIVE _____
_____
_____

I, _____, FORGIVE _____
_____
_____

I, _____, FORGIVE _____
_____
_____

I, _____, FORGIVE _____
_____
_____

I, _____, FORGIVE _____
_____
_____

I, _____, FORGIVE _____
_____
_____

Listening is a magnetic and strange thing, a creative force. The friends who listen to us are the ones we move toward. When we are listened to, it creates us, makes us unfold and expand.

—Karl A. Menninger

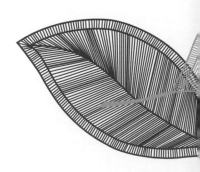

The Value of Listening

Despite all the technological ways to instantly transfer information to each other, people are self-reporting increased feelings of loneliness, isolation, and difficulties with communication. One of the most generous gifts we can give to anyone is to authentically and completely listen to them. This means to set aside or turn off any devices, stop multitasking, quiet the voices in our mind, and attentively listen.

Many of us believe we are great listeners, sometimes able to replay a conversation word for word. However, just because we can remember what's been spoken, it doesn't mean that the other person feels heard or that we actually understood what they were attempting to communicate. Being a generous listener means being totally present and thoughtfully considering someone else's perspective. It means listening like we would like others to listen to us.

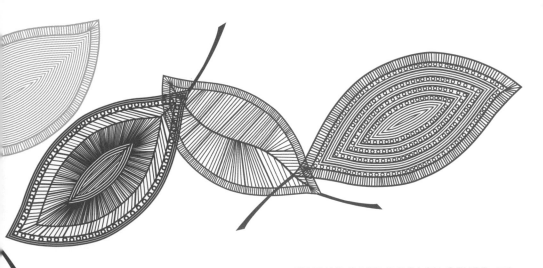

TOOLS FOR REAL LISTENING & UNDERSTANDING

Here are some tips to help you know when you've genuinely listened to the person you are in conversation with:

CLUES FROM THE OTHER PERSON:

1) The other person feels heard.
2) The other person's voice gets more attention from you than the voice in your head.
3) The other person doesn't feel the need to repeat themselves.
4) The other person says thank you or shows appreciation.
5) The other person is aware of how long they are speaking.
6) The other person feels good.

CLUES FROM YOURSELF:

1) You aren't paying attention to how much time is passing.
2) You aren't focusing on your own response or anything else.
3) You aren't thinking about who is right or wrong.
4) You can understand the other person's perspective even if you disagree.
5) You haven't interrupted.
6) You feel good.

Here are some tips to help you make it easier for the other person to listen to you:

1) Ask if this is a good time to talk. If it's not, set up a time.

2) Let the other person know what you are looking for in the conversation; for example, you may be looking for comfort, support, ideas, or just to be heard. Keep complaining to a minimum.

3) Phrase things positively.

4) Talk about how you feel.

5) Check in with the other person, and ask how they are doing.

6) Focus on solutions versus dissecting problems.

7) Notice if in your speaking you are criticizing or making the other person wrong.

8) Express appreciation and say thank you!

*Act as if what you do
makes a difference. It does.*
—William James

The Benefits of Service

Assisting others and engaging in something that is bigger than ourselves provides purpose in our lives. When we give to others from the heart, we receive just as much in return. Unexpected joy breaks through even during the most challenging times to keep us going.

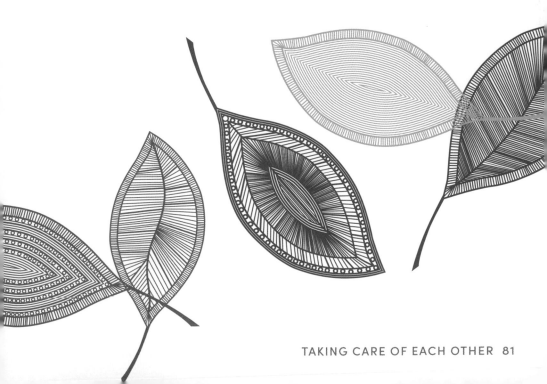

SIMPLE ACTS OF KINDNESS

Together, make a list of acts of kindness that you do for each other.

-
-
-
-
-
-
-
-
-
-

SIMPLE ACTS OF KINDNESS

In this family exercise, check off the emotions that describe how you feel after being the unexpected recipient of an unexpected act of kindness.

WE FEEL...

- ☐ Like singing
- ☐ Lighthearted
- ☐ Seen
- ☐ Important
- ☐ Special
- ☐ Cheerful
- ☐ Confident
- ☐ Lucky
- ☐ Happy
- ☐ Grateful
- ☐ Loved
- ☐ Like each of us matters
- ☐ Joyful
- ☐ Like dancing

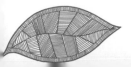

CONTRIBUTIONS WE MADE TO OTHERS

List ways you have helped family members, friends, neighbors, and others.

-
-
-
-
-
-
-
-
-

CONTRIBUTIONS WE MADE TO OTHERS

-

-

-

-

-

-

-

-

-

-

OUR VOLUNTEER WORK

Record all the many ways your family volunteers in your communities.

-
-
-
-
-
-
-
-
-
-

OUR VOLUNTEER WORK

-
-
-
-
-
-
-
-
-

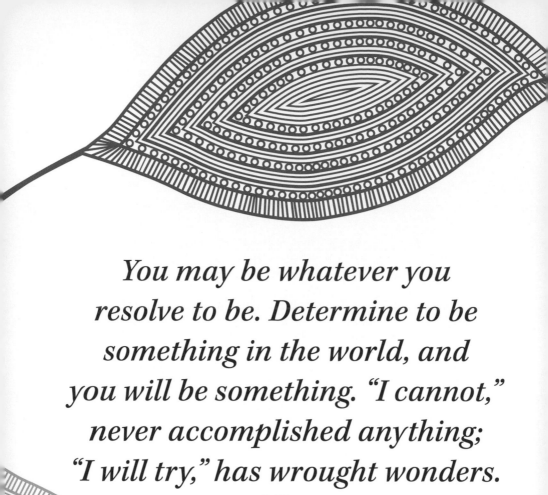

You may be whatever you resolve to be. Determine to be something in the world, and you will be something. "I cannot," never accomplished anything; "I will try," has wrought wonders.

—J. Hawes

OUR FAMILY'S MISSION STATEMENT

A family's mission statement describes a family's values, goals, and purpose.

In this section, you'll create your family's mission statement to inspire and direct your family as it grows. The statement can be long or short—whatever works best for your family. Family members should provide input and use it as a guide in their lives.

This mission statement is a living document, so update it, change it, and revise it to reflect your family as time passes. Keep a copy of your family's mission statement in your home where all of you can see it.

Your family's mission statement is an encapsulation of what your family believes is important. It lays out your shared focus and defines your purpose. It helps articulate the essence of your family.

Begin with identifying your shared values. List five values that best express who you are. There is additional space if you'd like to add more values.

OUR VALUES ARE

1) _____

2) _____

3) _____

4) _____

5) _____

_____

_____

_____

_____

_____

Next, identify your shared goals and your family's purpose. List your top five goals and state your family's purpose.

OUR SHARED GOALS ARE

1) _____

2) _____

3) _____

4) _____

5) _____

OUR PURPOSE IS

_____

_____

_____

_____

_____

_____

FAMILY'S MISSION STATEMENT DRAFT

Create your first version of your mission statement. Write, rewrite, add, erase, and scratch things out as you work on your statement. Capture your final version on the next page.

_____

_____

_____

_____

_____

_____

_____

_____

_____

_____

_____

_____

_____

_____

_____

_____

THE _____ FAMILY'S
MISSION STATEMENT

DATE _____

_____

_____

_____

_____

_____

_____

_____

_____

_____

_____

_____

_____

_____

_____

_____

_____

_____

_____

_____

_____

_____

*They can because
they think they can.*

—Virgil

OUR VISIONS & DREAMS

*If someone believes in you,
and you believe in your
dreams, it can happen.*

—T.L. Rowe

Visioning Our Family's Future

This section is about creating the future you want for your family. So, close your eyes and think about what your family will be doing, where and how you will be interacting in the future. Picture the place where you are living, who is in school, where everyone is working, and most importantly how your family is connecting. Once you have agreed on the picture, write it down in the following pages. Use photos or drawings if you'd like to add more dimension to your vision.

OUR FAMILY, ONE YEAR FROM TODAY...

_____

_____

_____

_____

_____

_____

_____

_____

OUR FAMILY, FIVE YEARS FROM TODAY...

_____

_____

_____

_____

_____

_____

_____

_____

OUR FAMILY, TEN YEARS FROM TODAY...

_____

_____

_____

_____

_____

_____

_____

_____

OUR FAMILY, TWENTY YEARS FROM TODAY...

_____

_____

_____

_____

_____

_____

_____

_____

A true friend knows your weaknesses but shows you your strengths; feels your fears but fortifies your faith; sees your anxieties but frees your spirit; recognizes your disabilities but emphasizes your possibilities.

—William Arthur Ward

Our Family's Support System

Ask anyone who has ever achieved their dreams and they will tell you about all the people who supported them along the way. Here is a place to identify all those people and organizations that have helped your family in the past, and those that will help your family in the future. They can be friends, relatives, coworkers, neighbors, teachers, and the clergy. Look around and see who is in your family's life.

PEOPLE WHO LISTEN TO US AND OUR IDEAS

-
-
-
-
-
-
-
-
-

PEOPLE WHO TELL US "YOU CAN DO IT"

-
-
-
-
-
-
-
-
-
-

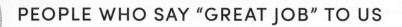

PEOPLE WHO SAY "GREAT JOB" TO US

-
-
-
-
-
-
-
-
-
-

PEOPLE WHO WE TRUST TO CALL WHEN WE REALLY NEED SUPPORT

-
-
-
-
-
-
-
-
-

ORGANIZATIONS WE BELONG TO BECAUSE WE WANT TO

-
-
-
-
-
-
-
-
-
-

PLACES WHERE WE GO WHEN WE WANT TO FEEL GOOD

-
-
-
-
-
-
-
-
-
-

PEOPLE, PLACES, AND THINGS THAT MAKE US SMILE

-

-

-

-

-

-

-

-

-

PEOPLE, PLACES, AND THINGS THAT MAKE US SMILE

-
-
-
-
-
-
-
-
-

You see things;
you say, "Why?"
But I dream things
that never were;
and I say, "Why not?"
—George Bernard Shaw

Our Family Strategy & Tools

Now that you have a clear vision for your family, what do you do with it?

This section provides steps to incorporate your vision into your family's life now.

Identify actions you can take as a family and as individuals in the next two weeks in support of the family's mission statement.

-
-
-
-
-
-
-
-
-
-

List resiliency building practices that your family will incorporate into daily life that also support the family's mission statement.

-
-
-
-
-
-
-
-
-
-

In one year, can you imagine together what will have happened in your family's life as a result of the family's mission statement?

_____

_____

_____

_____

_____

_____

_____

_____

_____

_____

_____

_____

_____

_____

_____

_____

_____

TO FOLLOW OUR MISSION STATEMENT, WE WILL

1) _____

_____

2) _____

_____

3) _____

_____

4) _____

_____

5) _____

_____

*Life without love is like a tree
without blossoms or fruit.*

—Khalil Gibran

EXPRESSIONS OF OUR LOVE

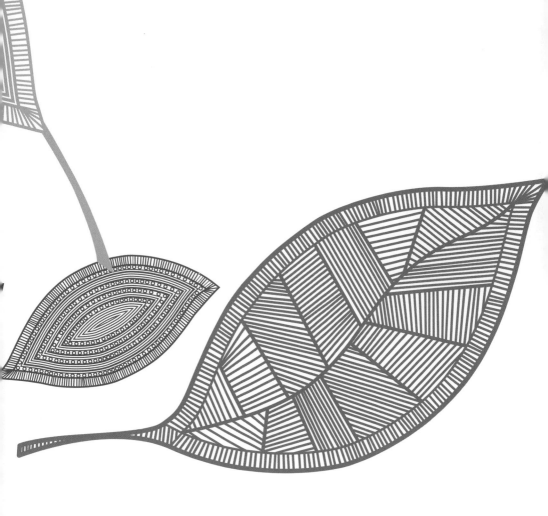

Love Lines

There is never too much giving and receiving love. Unfortunately, in our busy lives we often forget to tell those we care about just how much they mean to us. These two pages have some kind thoughts that you can use to share with each other. Select five statements every day and express those statements to your loved ones and to yourself to build connection, as individuals and as a family.

I appreciate you.

I really appreciate all you do for me.

I appreciate your generosity.

I appreciate your support.

I appreciate your kindness.

I appreciate your patience.

I appreciate your sense of humor.

I appreciate your love.

I love you.

I admire you.

I missed you.

You bring out the best in me.

You give the best hugs.

You are my role model.

You get me.

You inspire me.

You are the best.

You are the light in my life.

You are amazing.

You are my rock.

You are everything to me.

Thank you for being there for me.

Thank you for believing in me.

Thank you for doing everything you do.

Thank you for caring enough about me to say no.

Thank you for understanding.

Thank you for trusting me.

Thank you being you.

Thank you for loving me just the way I am.

Thank you for making me laugh.

Letter to Our Family

This final page is for you as a family to write a letter to yourselves to be read one year from today. Write from your heart. Share what you as a family are appreciative of and grateful for from the past year. Write about what you are looking forward to over the next year. Most importantly, thank each other for all the love you have shared.

LETTER TO OUR FAMILY

_____

_____

_____

_____

_____

_____

_____

_____

_____

_____

_____

_____

_____

_____

_____

_____

_____

_____

_____

_____

As I sit at life's seaside,
At times no human soul seems near
The waves they wash beside me
They are companions near and dear.

The soft sands warm my meeting
Each white cloud smiling sends
A glad message and warmest greeting
I am not really alone, but with friends.

I think of my family, whomever they may be
Remembering its love like a grain of sand
It's then I realize whatever confronts me
I'll win, because I feel their helping hands.

—Gene Tackowiak, U.S. Navy, 1940–1944

Recommended Reading

Arrien, Angeles. *Living in Gratitude: A Journey That Will Change Your Life.* Boulder, Colorado: Sounds True, 2011.

Begley, Sharon. *Train Your Mind, Change Your Brain: How a New Science Reveals Our Extraordinary Potential to Transform Ourselves.* New York: Ballantine, 2007.

Breuning, Loretta G. *The Science of Positivity.* Avon, Massachusetts: Adams, 2017.

Doidge, Norman. *The Brain That Changes Itself: Stories of Personal Triumph from the Frontiers of Brain Science.* New York: Penguin, 2007.

Emmons, Robert A. *Thanks! How the New Science of Gratitude Can Make You Happier.* Boston: Houghton Mifflin, 2007.

Emmons, Robert A. and Michael E. McCullough. *The Psychology of Gratitude.* New York: Oxford University Press, 2004.

Goleman, Daniel and Richard J. Davidson. *Altered Traits: Science Reveals How Meditation Changes Your Mind, Brain, and Body.* New York: Penguin, 2017.

Greitens, Eric. Resilience: *Hard-Won Wisdom for Living a Better Life.* New York: Houghton Mifflin, 2015.

Hanson, Rick and Forrest Hanson. *Resilient: How to Grow an Unshakable Core of Calm, Strength, and Happiness.* New York: Penguin, 2018.

Siegel, Daniel J. and Tina Payne Bryson. *The Yes Brain: How to Cultivate Courage, Curiosity, and Resilience in Your Child.* New York: Random House, 2018.

Zolli, Andrew and Ann Marie Healy. *Resilience: Why Things Bounce Back.* New York: Business Plus, 2012.

Acknowledgments

My deepest gratitude to the following people, who without their support I would never have undertaken this project. First, my family, my family is always first. Darryl and Christian, thank you for your unshakable belief in my healing and for believing that I could write these journals in such a short span of time even with my health limitations. Knowing you were there for me at every twist and turn made it possible for me to fulfill my dream of sharing this life-altering information with as many people as possible. I am so grateful.

Thank you to all my teachers during this twenty-four-year healing journey. I am truly at a loss for words to describe the depth of my appreciation for always being there to instruct and assist me. To my yoga teacher, you took me on as a student when I could barely move at times. I will always remember the dignity and respect with which you treat me as I continue work on my recovery. To Pam Lanza and Glenn Hirsch, who helped me find, connect, acknowledge, and own both my inner and outer artist when I didn't know I had either. I miss you both, may you rest in peace.

I am grateful for my many friends, colleagues, and neighbors who have stood with me during these many challenging years, enthusiastically encouraging my writing and my art. My dear friend Faith, who told me this was going to happen. I will celebrate with you in my heart. Aiko Morioka and Cathy River, who provided wise, compassionate counsel as I wrote these books. Thank you to Glenn Hartelius, Gordon Sumner, Laurie McFarlane, Karen Leveque, Matt Schwartz, John Kirkpatrick, and Debra Levin for supporting me in so many different ways. I also want to thank the many people around the world who trust me with their joys, fears, accomplishments, hurts, and their hearts. I am honored to be of service to you!

Thank you to those of you who literally these books would not exist without your stellar work. To Luke Schwartz, research assistant extraordinaire for expanding and coordinating my twenty-plus years of research and resources. To the amazing team at West Margin Press, I am so grateful for all of you. To Jen Newens for understanding my vision and providing the platform for this information to reach so many others. To Olivia Ngai for your detailed, precise, and tireless editing. To Rachel Metzger for your thoughtful, innovative designs and your open collaboration. Angie Zbornik for your strategic marketing ideas, innovative execution, and support. I deeply appreciate each and every one of you. Thank you!

ABOUT THE AUTHOR

Janine Wilburn is an award-winning artist, innovator, and writer. She has a master's degree in East West Psychology and is pursuing her PhD. For decades, Janine worked as a marketing professional, receiving recognition for her work with a Cannes Film Festival Bronze Lion, a Clio, and other awards, until a car accident changed her life. Suffering spinal damage, she needed to heal. Through her studies in neuroscience, neuroplasticity, yoga, and meditation, Janine persevered and developed resilience-building practices. The Resiliency Guides are the result of her research, experience, hope, and commitment to help others. Janine lives in San Francisco, California.

I dedicate this journal to my loving family.

This book is not intended to diagnose or replace any medical advice or information. The publisher and author do not make any warranties about the completeness, reliability, or accuracy of the information in these pages. The publisher and author are not responsible and are not liable for any damages or negative consequences from any treatment, action, or application to any person reading or following the information in this book.

Art Credits: Koru by Kate Bourke from the Noun Project; leaves by Yuliya Koldovska/Shutterstock.com

ISBN: 9781513264431

Printed in China
1 2 3 4 5

Published by West Margin Press

WEST
MARGIN
PRESS
WestMarginPress.com

Proudly distributed by Ingram Publisher Services

WEST MARGIN PRESS
Publishing Director: Jennifer Newens
Marketing Manager: Angela Zbornik
Editor: Olivia Ngai
Design & Production: Rachel Lopez Metzger